ANIMALS WITHOUT BRAINS!

SEA ANEMONES ARE BRAINLESS!

By Amanda Vink

Gareth Stevens PUBLISHING

Please visit our website, www.garethstevens.com. For a free color catalog of all our high-quality books, call toll free 1-800-542-2595 or fax 1-877-542-2596.

Library of Congress Cataloging-in-Publication Data

Names: Vink, Amanda, author.
Title: Sea anemones are brainless! / Amanda Vink.
Description: New York : Gareth Stevens Publishing, [2020] | Series: Animals without brains! | Includes index.
Identifiers: LCCN 2019020400| ISBN 9781538245866 (paperback) | ISBN 9781538245880 (library bound) | ISBN 9781538245873 (6 pack)
Subjects: LCSH: Sea anemones–Juvenile literature.
Classification: LCC QL377.C7 V56 2020 | DDC 593.6–dc23
LC record available at https://lccn.loc.gov/2019020400

Published in 2020 by
Gareth Stevens Publishing
111 East 14th Street, Suite 349
New York, NY 10003

Designer: Sarah Liddell
Editor: Amanda Vink

Photo credits: Cover, pp. 1, 11, 15 Ethan Daniels/Shutterstock.com; background used throughout Sanjatosic/Shutterstock.com; p. 5 Maurizio Biso/Shutterstock.com; p. 7 Cegli/Shutterstock.com; p. 9 Spiroview Inc/Shutterstock.com; p. 13 Charlotte Bleijenberg/Shutterstock.com; p. 17 Offscreen/Shutterstock.com; p. 19 SergeUWPhoto/Shutterstock.com; p. 21 Shahar Shabtai/Shutterstock.com.

Printed in the United States of America

CPSIA compliance information: Batch #CW20GS: For further information contact Gareth Stevens, New York, New York at 1-800-542-2595.

CONTENTS

A Sea Flower 4
The Invertebrate Family 6
Around the World 8
Life As a Sea Anemone 10
Deadly Hunter 12
Regeneration 16
Friendly Relationships 18
Doing Their Job 20
Glossary 22
For More Information 23
Index 24

Boldface words appear in the glossary.

A Sea Flower

Sea anemones are named after a flowering plant. They look like one too! But sea anemones aren't flowers. They're living animals. You may be surprised to learn that sea anemones don't have brains! How do they stay alive?

The Invertebrate Family

Sea anemones are part of the animal family called invertebrates. Members of this family don't have backbones or bony **skeletons**. Invertebrates are the largest group in the animal kingdom, about 97 percent of all animals!

Around the World

More than 1,000 species, or kinds, of sea anemones live throughout the world's oceans. Sea anemones can grow up to 6 feet (1.8 meters). They come in a **variety** of colors and fix themselves to rocks with a single foot called a basal disc.

Life As a Sea Anemone

Sea anemones have a single opening that acts as mouth, which is bordered by **tentacles**. Some have a few hundred tentacles! A sea anemone has radial symmetry. That means if a sea anemone were cut in half, both sides would look the same.

Deadly Hunter

Sea anemones are **carnivores**. They eat tiny **plankton**. Because they don't have brains, sea anemones must hunt for their food in **unique** ways! Sea anemones have a nerve net, which allows for **complex** muscle movement.

When a sea anemone feels prey touch it, the sea anemone knows food is nearby. When prey comes near, a sea anemone's tentacle shoots poison into it. The sea anemone uses its tentacles to pull food into its mouth.

Regeneration

Sea anemones bodies are amazing! They have special cells not all animals have. Because of these cells, sea anemones can **regenerate**. If they are cut in half, two separate, identical creatures are created.

Friendly Relationships

Sea anemones and clownfish have a symbiotic relationship, which means they help one another. Clownfish have a protective mucous coating that allows them to live inside the anemone. They help to keep the anemone clean!

Doing Their Job

Sea anemones keep more than just clownfish safe. They also keep a number of other marine life, such as shrimp and crab, safe. Sea anemones help keep the ocean **diverse**. They don't need a brain to accomplish this job!

GLOSSARY

carnivore: an animal that eats meat

complex: having to do with something with many parts that work together

diverse: differing from each other

plankton: a tiny plant or animal that floats in the ocean

regenerate: to grow (as a lost body part) once more

skeleton: the bony frame of the body

tentacle: one of the long thin flexible parts that stick out around the head or the mouth of an animal

unique: one of a kind

variety: a collection of different things

FOR MORE INFORMATION

BOOKS

Magby, Meryl. *Under the Sea: Sea Anemones.* New York, New York: PowerKids Press, 2012.

Rake, Jody S. *Sea Anemones (Faceless, Spineless, and Brainless Ocean Animals).* North Mankato, Minnesota: Capstone Press, 2017.

WEBSITES

Ducksters: Invertebrates
www.ducksters.com/animals/invertebrates.php
This website features information about all invertebrates.

National Geographic: Sea Anemones
www.nationalgeographic.com/animals/invertebrates/group/sea-anemones/
Featuring beautiful photography, this website lists sea anemone statistics.

INDEX

carnivore 12

cell 16

clownfish 18, 20

crustaceans 20

diverse 20

flower 4

mouth 10, 14

mucous 18

muscle 12

nerve net 12

ocean 8, 20

plankton 12

plant 4

poison 14

regenerate 16

skeleton 6

symmetry 10

tentacle 10, 14